Li…

GAGS

Dorothy Freund

Michael O'Mara Humour

First published in Great Britain in 2001 by
Michael O'Mara Books Limited
9 Lion Yard, Tremadoc Road
London SW4 7NQ

A CIP catalogue record for this book is available from the British Library

ISBN 1-85479-590-2

1 3 5 7 9 10 8 6 4 2

Designed and typeset by K DESIGN

www.mombooks.com

Printed in Australia by McPherson's Printing Group

INTRODUCTION

Following Frank Freund's fatal fall (or was he pushed?) from an airborne basket at the Greek monastery he had eventually entered, his doughty mother, Dorothy, has made it her life's work to get into print his planned publication – the book you now hold in your hands. She recalls that when Frank lived at home, he was forever closeted in his darkened room, with his floppies in one hand while pumping away on his hard drive with the other, cramming full of fun the disks that he was sure would add to the gaiety of nations.

A fully qualified stenographer herself, it was no time before Dorothy mastered the mysteries of the PC and of digital encryption. She was, for once, speechless at the material that flashed up on Frank's miracle monitor: disclosure on the sex life of Mickey Mouse's dog; the plight of the horizontally challenged budgerigar; how to tell if a lawyer's well hung; the pulling power of lesbians –

these are just a few of the mysteries contained in this resulting volume, tales that Frank is probably still recounting around that great Camp Fire in the Sky. As for Frank's own theory on whether gay men and women are conceived that way – 'Consider it a case of Divine Intervention' – this is just one of the awesome truths with which he left us. Truly a legacy of love and laughter.

Dorothy is especially grateful to the following, without whose help and encouragement Frank's life's work might never have seen the light of day: Charles, Tony, Jared, Catalina, Geoff, Ian, Tom, Bill, *les sœurs* Wapshott and, of course, Pru Pritchard.

KENNETH F. THOMSON
Webmaster & Friend of Dorothy Freund,
London and San Diego, February 2001

www.dorothy@thefriendsof.com

CAMP COMEDY

Rod's birthday party is in full swing when Kurt finds him huddled alone in a corner, quietly sobbing in deep despair.

'Oh, come on,' says Kurt soothingly. 'It's not that bad – you're only twenty-eight.'

'Twenty-eight,' sobs Rod. 'In gay years that makes me *sixty-eight*!'

Two gays are having a drink and one says to the other: ‘Guess what, I got circumcised a few weeks ago.’

‘Wow,’ says the other. ‘Do let me have a look!’

So the first guy pulls out his penis and displays it with some pride.

‘Oh boy,’ says his friend. ‘You look ten years younger!’

Did you hear about the two gay judges?

They decided to try each other.

How many gays does it take to mug a woman?

Four – three to hold her down and one to do her hair.

A drag queen was attending a Catholic Mass and when he saw the priest walking down the aisle in full religious get-up, swinging the incense burner, he called out:

'Love the dress, honey, but you'd better watch out – your purse is on fire!'

Freud certainly didn't have to be a genius to know that Michelangelo was gay – who else but a gay man would spend his whole life painting a ceiling?

One of the funniest scenes in all TV sitcom has to be in the brilliant '70s series *Soap*. In one climactic episode the mixed-up character Jodie, played by Billy Crystal, tries to explain to his mother Jessica (Katherine Helmond) why it's actually okay to be gay. In time-honoured fashion, he recites the names of some of the major gays in human history – Socrates, Michelangelo, Leonardo da Vinci, Oscar Wilde, Walt Whitman, Brahms, E.M. Forster, and so on. Everything's going fine till the name Plato is added to the list. *'Plato!'* gasps his mother. '*Plato?!* Mickey Mouse's dog is *gay?!*'

How many gay guys does it take to change a light bulb?

Seven – one to change the bulb and six to stand around saying 'Faaabulous'!

What do you call a gay bar with nowhere to sit?

A fruit stand.

How do you tell a straight crew in a boat race from a gay one?

In the straight crew, there's only one screaming.

How do you know when you've been burgled by gays?

The furniture's been rearranged and there's a quiche in the oven.

What do you call stray poodles?

Homo-less.

Kurt and Rod go to the funfair. Rod decides to take a ride on the Ferris wheel. He gets on and some minutes later there is a terrific crash. The wheel falls to the ground with an almighty noise and Rod is thrown off into a pile of rubble. Kurt rushes to him through the chaotic scene.

'Are you hurt, are you hurt?' he asks Rod, with great urgency.

'Hurt?' sobs Rod. 'I went round three times and you didn't wave *once*!'

A Jewish mother was talking to a friend:

'I have some good news and some bad news. The bad news is my son tells me he's gay. The good news? His boyfriend's a doctor.'

Which are the only bars that *always* have a strict dress code?
Transvestite bars.

Two queens arrived home in the early hours after a hot night's clubbing to find that they'd lost their front-door keys. After some panicked and high-pitched whispering one of them spotted that a bedroom window had been left open, and the other that a ladder had been left lying in the side passage.

As they climbed to safety one said, 'Oooh, doesn't this make you feel like a fireman?!'

'Sure does,' replied the other, 'but where would you find one at this time of night?'

There was this Jewish boy, and his father says to him, 'Maurice, you're not yourself today, you're acting in a very strange way. What's the problem?'

'It's okay. I'm all right, Father,' came the glum reply.

'I know what's happened,' his father went on, 'you've gone to the country estate, you've had a party, things got out of hand and the place burned down . . . Not to worry, the insurance will take care of everything.'

'No, I haven't been to the country estate, Father; I'm perfectly all right.'

'So perhaps you took the yacht out

with some friends – there's been a fire on the yacht, or you've sunk the yacht, who knows? The maritime insurance covers all of that. Just don't worry about it.'

'No, Father, I haven't taken the yacht out.'

'Well, what is it my son?'

'Well, if you insist on knowing, Father, I'm gay.'

'Gay? Gay?' replies the father. 'Try it for a fortnight and if you like it we'll buy a boys' school.'

What's safe sex?

When you live in London and your boyfriend lives in Glasgow.

What's the bravest thing you can think of?

Two cannibals having oral sex.

What do you call a pack of queer lions?

Gay pride.

Graffiti: My mother made me a homosexual.

Written underneath: If I get her the wool will she make me one too?

Graffiti: I am 6 inches in circumference and 9 inches long.

Written underneath: Very interesting – but how big is your cock?

Is it better being black or gay?
Black – you don't have to explain to your mother.

Kurt is away on business and Rod decides to make do with a vibrator. Unfortunately, it gets stuck and, with great embarrassment, he goes to the doctor.

'To remove that,' says the doctor, 'I'm going to have to perform a very long and delicate operation.'

'I don't think I can afford that,' replies Rod. 'Could you just replace the batteries?'

Did you hear about the gay Roman Catholic?
He couldn't make up his mind if the Pope was faaabulous or just simply divine.

And what about the gay Bible?
The first couple were Adam and Steve.

How do you know if you're in a gay church?
Only half the congregation are on their knees.

A tourist from Azerbaijan goes on an overseas trip and is obviously puzzled trying to fill in a visa application. An immigration official looks over his shoulder and sees that the tourist is writing in 'Twice a week' in the box labelled 'SEX'. The official explains that that is not what is meant by the question.

'We are asking "MALE" or "FEMALE",' he says.

'Doesn't matter,' answers the tourist.

❁

A man was up before the court for raping one of the boys from the

Barnsbury Boys' Brass Band.

'What is the prisoner in the dock accused of?' asked the presiding judge.

To which the prosecuting barrister replied: 'The prisoner in the dock, Your Honour, is accused of raping one of the boys from the Barnsbury Boys' Brass Band.'

The judge immediately brought down his gavel with a curt 'Case dismissed!'

'But,' protested the prosecutor, 'you haven't heard the case.'

'No,' said the judge, 'but I have heard the Barnsbury Boys' Brass Band, and I think they all ought to be fucked!'

Did you hear about the gay travelling salesman?

He had a false bottom in his suitcase.

What kind of lubricant do racists use?

KKK-Y jelly.

What's the name of a show about gay cowboys?

Okla-homo.

Three young men presented themselves at a monastery as candidates for the monastic order. A stern old monk delivered a lecture to them on the privations of life in the monastery and then ushered them into a room, explaining that they had to take an important preliminary test before they could be put forward as candidates.

When they had stripped naked, he tied a little bell to their penises, and then left them. The next time the door opened, a beautiful, bikini-clad young woman walked in. Moments later she exited to the sound of one tinkling bell.

Realizing he'd failed the test, the young man shouted: 'Oh please, please, give me another chance.' But when the door opened again, the woman was completely naked and the bell rang even more energetically.

'I'm very sorry, but you have demonstrated that the monastic life is not for you,' said the monk, who'd been listening through a chink in the wall. 'I must ask you to leave.'

Desolated, the young man bent down to collect his bundle of clothes.

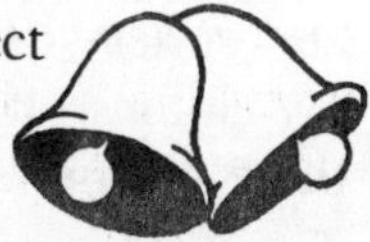

And two other bells went crazy.

A gay man goes to the doctor and complains that his partner is losing interest in sex. The doctor gives him a pill and, with the warning that it is still in its experimental, trial stage, tells him to crush it up and slip it into his friend's dinner that evening.

A week later he's back at the doctor's: 'The pill was great! It really worked. I put it into his vegetables and it wasn't five minutes before he jumps up, throws all the food, dishes, and cutlery to the floor, grabs me, rips my clothes off and ravishes me right there on the table!'

'Oh dear,' says the doctor. 'I'm very sorry – I had no idea the pill was that strong! The medical foundation will be glad to pay for any damages.'

'No, it doesn't matter in the least,' says the patient. 'We won't be going back to that restaurant anyway.'

What's the difference between normal poker and gay poker?

In gay poker the queens are wild and no straights are allowed.

A senior Roman Catholic priest was summoned to the Vatican for a three-week conference. Unfortunately, there was no one to take his place in his absence except a very young priest with no experience whatsoever.

'I feel up to the challenge,' the young priest assured his superior, 'but I'm not totally sure how to manage the confessional. What penance do I prescribe for the various sins that I'm sure to be confronted with?'

The older priest left him a list of penances matched to sins for his reference and, giving the young man his blessing, set off for Rome.

Before he knew it, the young priest's first confessional was upon him and he stepped nervously into the booth, armed with the list he had been left by his predecessor.

'Forgive me Father, for I have sinned. I, a married man, have had impure thoughts about a woman I work with,' came the first voice.

The young priest scanned his list: 'Impure thoughts: *see also* Adulterous thoughts, Disrespectful thoughts, Murderous thoughts,' he read.

He looked up 'Adulterous thoughts' and saw that four Hail Marys were in order. Relieved, he prescribed the penance and waited for the next sinner.

'Forgive me Father, for I have sinned,' came the voice through the grate. 'I took £50 from the office cash box which was not mine.'

'Stealing: £10 – 10 Hail Marys; £100 – 20 Hail Marys; £1,000 – 50 Hail Marys; £10,000 – 80 Hail Marys,' the priest found in his list. His confidence was growing as he prescribed the appropriate penance and he settled down to await the next confessor.

'Forgive me Father, for I have sinned: I was given a blow job by another man. And I enjoyed it.'

The priest checked the list again. Of

course, 'Blow job' wasn't included and, to his dismay, nor was 'Fellatio'; and there was no reference to any similar activity, either. 'Homosexual experience' wasn't even mentioned, and he couldn't find anything under 'Sucking', 'Oral sex', 'Mouth', 'Lips', 'Penis', or other relevant anatomical parts. In a panic, he thrust his head from the box and grabbed hold of a choirboy, who just happened to be walking past.

'Tell me, what does the priest give for a blow job?' he asked urgently.

'Oh, sometimes a Mars Bar, sometimes a KitKat,' the boy answered, and went on his way.

BISEXUAL BANTER

Bisexual men are easy to please – they like the girls as well as the next guy.

One sure thing about being bisexual – it doubles your chances of being without a date for Saturday night.

A new addition to the office is taken out by one of his new workmates for an after-work get-to-know-you drink. They go to a bar where the first man spots an obviously gay couple chatting away and having a fine old time.

'I don't know about this gay thing,' says he. 'I don't think I could get into it, could you?'

'Well,' says the newcomer, 'I think a *bisexual* experience might be worth a try.'

'Really?' says the first man, his mouth dropping open with surprise.

'Sure,' says the other, 'but only if I could find the right woman.'

THE
GAIETY OF NATIONS

Did you hear about the Irish lesbian?
She liked men.

And the two contented Irish gays?
Patrick Fitzwilliam and William Fitzpatrick.

Did you hear about the man who moved to San Francisco?

He turned prematurely gay.

How many straight San Francisco men does it take to change a light bulb?

Both of them.

San Francisco has its own patron saint: St Francis the Sissy. His miracle was changing breakfast into brunch.

❁

What do they call gays in the Southern States of America?

Homosex-you-alls.

❁

What do fishermen and Mexican gays have in common?

They're always going on about 'The Juan that got away'.

In Greece, how do they separate the men from the boys?

With a crowbar.

What do you get if you cross an Italian and a gay?

A Sissylian.

What did the bisexual German woman do?

She went down on her Hans and niece.

Why do Scotsmen wear kilts?
Because sheep can hear a zip from miles away.

A Scot at the Gay Highland Games recently set a world record:
Mr Hamish Cameron was the winner, with 226 feet, in the salad-tossing event.

Four men survive a plane crash in the wastes of the Arctic Circle. Eventually one of them dies, and the other three decide they'll have to eat him to stand any chance of surviving.

'I'm from Hartlepool,' pipes up one of the men. 'I'll eat his heart.'

'And I'm from Liverpool,' says the next man. 'I'll go for the liver.'

'Well, I'm from Cockfosters,' says the third, 'and I'm not hungry.'

A homophobic Knightsbridge matron was propounding her views to another, rather nicer, woman at a cocktail party.

'It's ghastly,' she said. 'They're everywhere now, even in government. Unnatural, if you ask me. I've no time for them at all – as far as I'm concerned you could put them all on an island in the Pacific and drop a bomb on them.'

'Good Heavens, dear,' replied her friend. 'I should so hate Harrods being turned into a self-service!'

What do you call an Iraqi with a sheep under one arm and a goat under the other?

Bisexual.

A stagecoach is travelling through the Australian bush when suddenly a gang of bushrangers springs out in front of it. 'Stop! I'm Ned Kelly. We're going to rob the women and rape the men!' says the leader.

'Er, Ned, don't you mean rob the men and rape the women?' asks one of his men.

Then a camp male voice issues from within the stagecoach:

'Who's robbing this stagecoach, you or Mr Kelly?'

Australia's first lady, Dame Edna Everage, was in Melbourne when there was an outbreak of garden gnomes being stolen from people's homes.

Asked for a comment, Dame Edna replied: 'These are sick, sick people to wreck beautiful Australian gardens – nothing more than gnomosexuals!'

Q: What's the difference between a Qantas steward and a washing machine?

(Now stand, swivel your hips and – in an opposite direction – swing your arms quickly, forearms at right angles to the body, wrists limp, first quickly in a clockwise, then an anti-clockwise direction.)

A: Not a lot.

FAIRY FARCE

Some favourite gay operas: *Dildo and Aeneas*, *The Fairy Queen*, *Oedipoof Rex*, *The Flying Butch-man*, *Ariadne auf Lesbos*, *Doris Godunov*, *Cav and Fag*, *The Fairies*, *Porgy and Seth*, *Fagoletto*.

Liberace, Freddie Mercury and Princess Diana all turn up at the Pearly Gates at the same time. St Peter explains to them that currently he only has room for one and asks all three of them to justify their claims for entry into Heaven.

Liberace starts off: 'Well *I* deserve a place because in my time I was a great entertainer and gave pleasure to millions of people. I wore beautiful costumes that delighted the eye and gave lots of money to charity.'

'I too was hugely popular for my music-making and had followers in their millions throughout the world;

many charities benefited from my generosity – I think I should get into Heaven,' says Freddie.

At that, St Peter pronounces: 'Well, I'm sorry boys – Diana, you're in.'

'Why is that?' protest Liberace and Freddie.

'Well,' Peter explains, 'everyone knows that a royal flush beats two queens any time.'

Why do gays make unsatisfactory Santa Clauses?
They'd rather wear the stockings than fill them.

How do you make a fruit cordial?
Pat him on the bottom.

Why was the gay captain thrown out of the army?
For playing with his privates.

A little kid runs in after a day at school: 'Mummy, mummy, someone at school called me a sissy!'

'So what did you do, dear?' asks his mother.

'I hit him with my handbag!'

What do you get when you cross a rooster with a peanut-butter sandwich?

A cock that sticks to the roof of your mouth.

A man dies and ends up in Hell, where he is greeted by the Devil, who notices that the new arrival seems rather disconsolate.

DEVIL: Welcome to my domain. But tell me, why are you so sad?

MAN: Oh, come on, man – anyone would feel miserable on realizing he's been consigned to Hell for all time!

DEVIL: Well, just have another think: Hell can be a lot of fun! For instance, do you drink?

MAN: Always been one of my favourite pastimes – I love to drink.

DEVIL: Well, *Mondays* are for you then.

Because on Mondays all we do is drink. Beer, whisky, gin, rum, tequila, vodka – you name it, you can have as much as you like. We throw it back till we puke, and then we get stuck in again!

MAN: Sounds great to me.

DEVIL: And what about smoking?

MAN: Sure thing – damn right I smoke.

DEVIL: That's cool – you're gonna love *Tuesdays*: you'll have the finest cigars from all over the world, and as many cigarettes as you can take. Smoke all you want, and you don't even have to worry about the health risks – you're dead already!

MAN: Wow, roll on Tuesdays.

DEVIL: What about gambling – you like that?

MAN: Sure, can't get enough.

DEVIL: Okay, that's *Wednesdays* taken care of. In Hell that's gambling night – slot machines, roulette, craps, blackjack, horse racing, poker and every kind of card game you have and haven't heard of.

MAN: Can't wait – Wednesdays sound fun.

DEVIL: And how about getting stoned?

MAN: Can't beat it – you mean, down here . . .

DEVIL: That's right, man, because on *Thursday* it's stoner night here in Hell! Help yourself, gratis, to huge rocks of crack, smoke the biggest joint you ever dreamed of. Do all the drugs you fancy without worrying about overdosing – because now you're dead anyway!

MAN: Wild! I had no idea Hell was such a swinging place.

DEVIL: Are you gay?

MAN: Er, no, I'm not.

DEVIL: Oooh – you're gonna ***hate*** *Fridays*!

On the road on business one night, a salesman found that every hotel room in a small town was taken.

'Please, I need a room – or just a bed. I don't care where. I'm completely exhausted,' he pleaded to the manager of the last hotel.

'Well, there is a double room with just one occupant,' admitted the manager. 'And I know he'd be happy to split the cost. But I should tell you he snores so loudly that there have been complaints from the adjoining rooms, so I'm not sure you'd think it was worth it.'

'Done,' said the weary traveller. 'I'll take it.'

The next morning the guy came down for breakfast, bright-eyed and bushy-tailed. The manager asked him how he was and how he managed to survive.

'Never felt better,' came the reply.

'No problem with the other guy snoring then?'

'No, I shut him up in no time.'

'How'd you manage that?'

'Well, he was already in bed, snoring his head off when I came in the room,' said the traveller. 'I tiptoed over to him, kissed him on the cheek and said "Goodnight gorgeous" – and he sat up all night watching me.'

A gay man goes to his hairdresser in a state of shock. 'What's wrong with you?' asks the hairdresser.

'I don't know what to say – I've just found out that my older brother's gay too!'

'But last time you told me your *younger* brother was gay! Is there *no one* in your family that likes women?' asks the hairdresser.

'Oh, sure there is – my sister!'

What are gays' favourite three things?
To eat, drink and be Mary.

How can you tell if a priest is gay?
The way he says 'A-men'.

A man walks into a bar with a pet alligator on a lead. To the amazement of the patrons, he puts the alligator on the bar and says to the assembled drinkers: 'I'll make you an offer. I'll open this 'gator's mouth and place my genitals inside; he'll then close his mouth for one minute. If my bits and pieces are still intact when he opens his mouth, you'll all buy me a drink for the entertainment we've provided.'

The crowd murmurs approval and the man drops his trousers and pops his private parts into the alligator's mouth. The crowd gasp as the reptile closes its mouth and, after a minute has passed, the man grabs a beer bottle and taps the alligator on the head. And, sure enough, when the alligator responds by opening its mouth, the man's genitals are unscathed, much to the delight of the drinkers who start to pass him the promised booze. Having downed a couple of the drinks, the man stands up again to make another offer: 'I'll pay anyone who's willing to try the same trick.'

A hush fell over the bar, till a young queen pushed forward.

'I'll try, but only if you promise not to hit me on the head with the bottle.'

'Daddy, Daddy, what's a transvestite?'
'Shut up son, and unhook my bra!'

Why are gays more careful drivers than straights?
If they have an accident the newspaper will print their age.

Why are gays better businessmen than straights?
They've got a better eye for the bottom line.

‘The vicar was walking in the garden of his vicarage when he came across a tiny frog. “Please will you do some-thing to help me?” asked the tiny frog.

‘“Certainly,” replied the vicar. “What would you like me to do?”

‘“Well, you see, I’m not really a frog, I’m really a lithe, young, blond man who’s been turned into a frog by a wicked witch.”

‘“How ghastly, no wonder you’re upset. How can we put things right?” asked the vicar.

‘“Well, if you take me home and put me on your pillow overnight, that might do the trick.”

‘And that, Your Honour, ends the case for the defence.’

It's a slow day in Metropolis and Superman is flying around thinking of something to do. He spots Spiderman and zooms down to him:

'Hi, Spiderman, what are you up to today?'

Spiderman reluctantly admits that he has a broken webslinger so he couldn't do anything. Superman flies on, only to spot Batman, and he asks the same question about his activities for the day.

'Nothing much,' says Batman. 'Just fixing the Batcar.'

Next on his travels, Superman sees Wonder Woman, lying naked on her back, legs apart, on top of a Metropolis skyscraper. Superman has a wicked thought – that if he were faster than the speeding train, he could zoom down and screw Wonder Woman before she knew what happened. So he flew down, screwed her faster than a speeding bullet and flew off.

'Hey! What happened?' exclaimed Wonder Woman, coming to her senses. And the Invisible Man rolled over: 'I sure don't know,' he replied, 'but my ass is killing me!'

A man was transferred by his firm to a remote town. It was very pleasant, but unfortunately for him there were no women in it. He looked around for weeks and finally found a bar on the outskirts of town. He was bemoaning the lack of sex to the barman.

'What do you do for pleasure around here?' he asked.

'No problem,' said the barman. 'See that box over in the corner, just stick your cock into the hole.'

So the man did exactly that and came back some minutes later.

'Wow, that was really good – when can I use that box?' he asked.

'Every day except Thursday,' replied the barman.

'Why, what's wrong with Thursday?' asked the man, perplexed.

'That's *your* day in the box,' explained the barman.

A screamer got on to a bus, to be confronted by a massive bus driver.

'Faggot,' he sneered. 'Where's your pearls?'

'*Pearls with corduroy*!' shrieked the gay. 'Are you out of your *mind*?!'

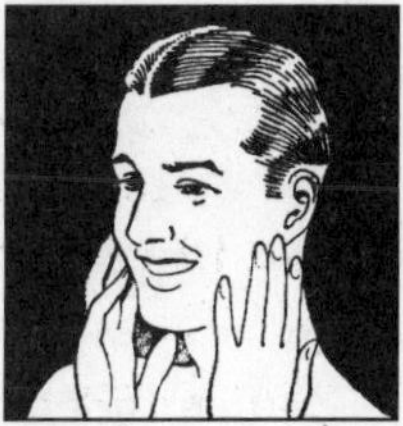

Why is a condom like a Kodak print?

They both capture that special moment.

A man goes into a public urinal and sees that the man standing next to him seems in a rather agitated state, just standing there flapping his hands around.

Poor guy, he thinks – probably got some debilitating disease.

'Can I help?' he asks solicitously.

'That's very kind,' says the other man. 'If you could just take my cock out for me I'd be most grateful.'

So the first man obliges, unzips the other man's trousers and takes his cock out and holds it while he has a piss.

Then he puts it back and zips the flies up again, saying, 'This must be terrible for you – do you always have this trouble?'

'Yes,' says the other. 'My nail polish always takes *such* a long time to dry!'

Did you hear about the gay king who wrote his autobiography?
It was a real page-turner.

What do you call two gays hanging on a wall?
Kurt 'n' Rod.

A fun game for gay guys to play with straight male friends:

Ask this question: 'If you woke up one morning in the middle of a field, covered with mud, in a terrible state, and with a used condom up your bottom, would you tell anyone?'

If the answer is 'Yes', the reply is: 'Well, you're not coming camping with *me*!'

If 'No', then you say: 'You can come camping with me *any time*.'

Barry and Bob are camping in the desert. While they are asleep in the tent, a snake slithers in and bites Bob on the prick. They both panic.

'What can we do?' they ask each other.

Then they decide that Bob should stay put while Barry races off to a nearby town to get some medical help. He finds the local doctor's office and runs past the receptionist to tell the doctor what happened.

'What kind of snake was it?' asks the doctor.

'About four feet long, sort of greenish-brown.'

'Oh, my God!' says the doc. 'Those critters are really dangerous – the only thing you can do is suck the poison out; otherwise, your friend will die.'

So, Barry hurries back to the tent and, to Bob's great surprise, starts packing his gear. 'Well,' asks Bob in anguish. 'What did the doctor say?!'

'He says you're going to die,' was Barry's swift reply.

QUEER QUIPS

As one sage put it, when asked whether gay men and lesbians are conceived that way 'No, consider it a case of Divine Intervention.'

Frank was so excited to be going bear-hunting. He spotted a small brown bear and shot it. Then there was a tap on his shoulder, and he turned around to see a big black bear.

The black bear said, 'You've got two choices. Either I maul you to death or we have sex.' Frank decided to bend over. Even though he felt sore for two weeks, Frank soon recovered and vowed revenge.

He headed out on another trip where he found the black bear and shot it. There was another tap on his shoulder. This time a huge grizzly bear stood right next to him.

The grizzly said, 'That was a huge mistake, Frank. You've got two choices. Either I maul you to death or we have rough sex.'

Again, Frank thought it was better to comply. Although he survived, it took several months before Frank finally recovered. Outraged, he headed back to the woods, managed to track down the grizzly and shot it. He felt sweet revenge, but then there was a tap on his shoulder. He turned round to find an even bigger grizzly bear standing there.

And the grizzly bear said, 'Come on Frank – admit it. You don't come here for the hunting, do you?'

A young queen goes into a bar and walks up to the barman.

'Excuse me,' he says. 'Are you the one they call Big Bull?'

'Yeah,' answers the barman. 'What's it to you?'

'Moooo!' comes the instant response.

Why do so many gays have moustaches?

To hide the stretch marks.

Two guys are walking along and they spot a contented dog lying in the sun, gently licking its genitals.

'Wow, I wish I could do that,' says one man.

'I'm sure he'd let you if you asked him nicely,' replies the other.

There's a new chain of gay bars called Boys-'R'-Us.

Rod is fed up because every time he goes to a local bar he's thrown out by the barman, who says: 'Get out, we don't want you faggy types here!'

After this has happened a few times, Rod thinks: 'Okay, I'll fix him.' And he goes home and borrows Kurt's military uniform, feeling very pleased with the overall butch effect.

However, Rod is appalled when he turns up in full military battledress only to have the barman say, once again: 'I told you, get out – we don't want your type here!'

Outside in the street, Rod is totally bewildered as to why he was ejected this time, so he checks his outfit in a mirror in a nearby shop window.

'Cap – fine; collar and tie – yes; epaulettes – correct; belt properly around the trousers; boots – bright and shiny like a proper soldier's.'

Then, to his mirrored image, he shrieks: '*Handbag*!'

Bob had had enough of the advertising business in Sydney, so he decided to pack it in and retire to the few thousand acres he'd bought in the outback, miles from anywhere.

After about six months of solitude, not having encountered a single other human being, he was sitting watching his satellite TV when he heard the roar of a motorbike pulling up at his front door. After a stentorian ring, he opened the door to find a tough-looking Aussie standing there.

'G'day,' the visitor said, 'the name's Bruce and I'm your nearest neighbour – about fifty miles away – and I reckoned it was time we met.'

'Nice to meet you,' said Bob, who was surprised at how pleased he was to clap eyes on another person after all this time.

'As a matter of fact,' Bruce went on, 'I'm throwing a party next Saturday night and I've driven over specially to invite you.'

'How nice,' said Bob, 'I'd love to come.'

'Good,' said Bruce, 'but I think I should warn you that there might be quite a lot of drinking going on.'

'That's okay with me,' replied Bob. 'After twenty-five years' practice in the advertising business I can hold my liquor.'

'And fighting – it can get a bit rough as the evening wears on.'

Bob thought to himself that he'd had enough experience in his old job, which had required him to get on smoothly with almost anybody. 'Fine, no problem,' he assured his host-to-be.

'Oh, and I should mention the sex,' added Bruce, 'there's sure to be some pretty wild sex at one of my parties.'

'Great,' thought Bob, after all these months alone this would be more than welcome. Then, as an afterthought, he asked: 'By the way, what about the dress code – what kind of clothes should I wear?'

'Oh, I wouldn't worry too much about that,' replied Bruce, 'there'll just be the two of us!'

A guy travelling on a bus spots a very attractive young nun. He tells the bus conductor how much he fancies her and asks if he knows anything about her.

'Well,' says the conductor, 'she's very devout and I know that at dawn every morning, without fail, she can be found in the field behind the church gathering flowers for the altar.'

This gives the guy an idea: next morning he dresses up as Jesus Christ and heads for the field where, sure enough, he finds the sister picking dew-covered flowers in the dim dawn light. He approaches the nun who throws up her hands in amazement and then adopts an attitude of great piety.

'My Lord,' she exclaims in a tiny voice racked with emotion, 'what a signal honour that You should appear here, to me of all people!'

'Please, think nothing of it,' says 'Jesus', 'but you can do one thing for me, my child.'

'Anything, my Lord, just ask it.'

'Well, now is the time to prove you really are the bride of Christ. I am in need of some physical release – I would like to have sex with you.'

'Of course, my Lord, I would – and must – do anything You ask,' replies the nun, 'but this is a difficult time of the month for me and I don't think I can manage it.'

'Never mind,' says 'Jesus', 'there is another way' – and he takes her from behind. As he is having sex with her, he feels a sudden pang of conscience to be taking such advantage of a holy woman. 'I have a terrible admission to make to you, sister,' he says to her, 'I am not really Jesus Christ.'

'Oh, that's all right,' says the other, 'I'm really a bus conductor!'

The residents of a small redneck town were urging the sheriff to arrest the local homosexual because he was continually propositioning the local male youth.

The sheriff dutifully made the arrest and said to him: 'Okay Mack, you've got fifteen minutes to blow this town!'

'Oh, for that I'll need at least two hours,' came the reply.

After quite a few beers in a bar, five guys start to argue about the size of their penises. Eventually the discussion turns into a full-blown argument, with each man insisting that his penis is the biggest.

'There's only one way to decide this,' says the barman. 'Let's have all your penises on the bar so we can compare.'

The drunks willingly comply. At that exact moment a queen enters the bar, looks around, and says to the barman: 'I think I'll have the buffet.'

A gay man visited the dentist to have a tooth extracted. After he had relaxed in the chair, the dentist approached him with a hypodermic, saying: 'You might just feel a little prick in your mouth at first.'

The patient smiled and said: 'Why, thank you!'

❀

A popular airline is Gay Air. The seating is 'screaming' or 'non-screaming', and when you assume the crash position you put your head between someone else's knees.

Why did Al Gore get the gay vote?
Because gays don't like Bush.

What do you call a vampire in drag?
A transvestbite.

How do you know if a lawyer's well hung?
If you can't get your thumb between the noose and his neck.

A priest and a minister walked into a bar. After sitting down and ordering drinks, the priest said: 'Have you noticed there are no women in here – I think we're in a gay bar.'

A man approached and tried to flirt with the priest, who was dumbfounded and didn't know what to do. Then the minister leaned over and whispered something in the man's ear. The man nodded and walked off.

The priest, greatly relieved, said: 'Thanks. What did you tell him?'

'I just told him we were on our honeymoon,' the minister replied.

Three gays were discussing the size of their boyfriends' penises.

The first one said: 'My George's is wonderful – about nine inches and smooth as silk.'

'Well, that's impressive, but my Bob's got eleven inches – circumcised and absolutely great,' said the second.

The third was rather quiet and one of the others asked him: '*Well*, what about your Buck then?'

'Oh, my Buck,' came the answer. 'Well, you know the budgerigars we have?'

'Yes,' chorused the others.

'All I can say is that when he's erect

I can stand fifteen budgerigars on it, side by side.'

'We don't believe you!' was the incredulous response.

'All right then – I must admit the one on the end *is* flapping its wings a bit!'

A couple of the contingents you see on the Gay Pride parade:

Gay cowboys – *fags on nags.*

Klondykes – *lesbians from the Yukon.*

Did you hear about the dog that was half pit bull terrier and half poodle?

It wasn't a good attack dog, but it was a vicious gossip.

Did you hear the one about the gay deaf-mute?

Neither did he.